FOLKS ON THE BLOCK RISE

Rev Attorney Dr. Theresa McCoy

Copyright © 2018 Rev Attorney Dr. Theresa McCoy.

Author Credits: I AM ESSAYS

All rights reserved. No part of this book may be used or reproduced by any means, graphic, electronic, or mechanical, including photocopying, recording, taping or by any information storage retrieval system without the written permission of the author except in the case of brief quotations embodied in critical articles and reviews.

Scripture taken from the King James Version of the Bible.

WestBow Press books may be ordered through booksellers or by contacting:

WestBow Press
A Division of Thomas Nelson & Zondervan
1663 Liberty Drive
Bloomington, IN 47403
www.westbowpress.com
1 (866) 928-1240

Because of the dynamic nature of the Internet, any web addresses or links contained in this book may have changed since publication and may no longer be valid. The views expressed in this work are solely those of the author and do not necessarily reflect the views of the publisher, and the publisher hereby disclaims any responsibility for them.

Any people depicted in stock imagery provided by Getty Images are models, and such images are being used for illustrative purposes only.
Certain stock imagery © Getty Images.

ISBN: 978-1-9736-2514-8 (sc)
ISBN: 978-1-9736-2515-5 (e)

Library of Congress Control Number: 2018904246

Print information available on the last page.

WestBow Press rev. date: 05/19/2018

DON'T KILL ME
God's Plan N

Contents

1. WHAT YOU SHOULD KNOW - DEFINITIONS AND MEANINGS TO PROPERLY INTERPRET WORDS AND THE WORLD YOU JOURNEYING THROUGH AT THIS TIME IN LIFE 1
2. SOMETHING TO SHARE THAT MAY HELP YOU GET A DIFFERENT PERSPECTIVE ON YOUR SITUATION 29
3. ABOUT ADOPTION AND BEING AN ADOPTIVE PARENT 51
4. THE MILLINIUM BUS TRIP 81
5. WHAT DOES IT ALL MEAN REALLY 82
6. REFERENCE 86

DEFINITIONS

On the block is where all
begins for most of us How we
talk
How we walk, socialize,
galvanize, visualize
Our expectations of
us and view of others begin ON THE BLOCK
IF YOU DARE TO READ, IT WILL
CHANGE EVERYTHING

The Block- my definition

Refers to a place where there is community; a group of people who have connected with one another in terms of social value, activity, family and protection from outsiders.

Note that when I googled the definition of "Block", (1) the definition herein was not found. Instead the "Block" was defined as 1. obstruction. 2. to obstruct. 3. regional anesthesia. ankle block regional anesthesia of the foot by injection ((3)Wikipedia -Block may refer to: Contents 1 Administrative subdivisions 2. Places 3. Objects 4. Science 5. Sports 6. Transport 7. Technology 8. Mathematics 9. Music 10. Broadcasting 11 .. and (2)Webster Dictionary's Definition of BLOCK. 1: a compact usually solid piece of substantial material especially when worked or altered to serve a particular purpose:

THIS BOOK IS WRITTEN FOR THE FOLKS ON THE BLOCK AS DEFINED AS A PLACE OF COMMUNITY, CONNECTION AND PROTECTION— BECAUSE I GREW UP ON THE BLOCK HEREIN REFERRED TO AS "AMES ST "LOCATED IN HAMMOND INDIANA

The Block Is Larger Than It Used To Be

IPHONES, INTERNET, KICS, IM, SMS, INSTAGRAMS FACEBOOK, LINKED-IN AND THE WHOLE DIGITAL MEDIA HAS OPENED WHAT USED TO BE AN ADDRESS IN CITIES TO GROUPS OF FOLK ALL OVER THE WORLD

Posting, sending photos, communicating whether with text, snapchat, or natural language the folk in the New and larger block get it. Everybody understands and shares what is going on. They talk about it, comment on it, sometimes defend an opinion, action or status. In the old block what happens in the larger Block may cause friction and violence or at least stir up negative emotions such as hatred and dislike.

"DON'T KILL
God's Plan N
ME"

As we enter the "Larger Block" remember this Mantra or thought

That which you seek you already are "begin with self-acceptance, opening with kindness to what is. "This compassionate quality wakes us up. We have more choices AND we are more connected than social media and are more alike than those naysayers would like us to believe.

Spiritual practice is about remembering who we are. When we encounter another human being and share or embrace their awareness, this encounter helps us to remember who we really are in the realm of humanity {because}they become our mirrors. Resting together in this energy called life. We should not be moved to create more violence in the world, or to violate ourselves." (4)Tara Brach, a psychologist and instructor of mindfulness practice)

Dedication

To my two daughters, Shanique Monique and Sherry Kathy Thomas AND Lakeisha Moore whom I call daughter, my God Daughters Adrienne Everette and Finalli Smith, my Nieces and Nephews that their thoughts be in line with the plans God the Creator of the Universe, God of Abraham Isaac and Jacob has for their lives and reveal in their lives the promise he gave (Micah 4:13 (3)Bible KJV)"Arise and thresh, O daughter of Zion: for I will make thine horn iron, and I will make thy hoofs brass: and thou shalt beat in pieces many people: and I will consecrate their gain unto the LORD, and their substance unto the Lord of the whole earth" AND for the Folks on the Block – where ever you live, West Side, South Side, East Side, South Burbs, Country, Across the Tracks, on the tracks, under the overpass, in the box, with foster parents, adopted parents, no parents, on drugs, recovering addict, recovering sinner, Saint (let's just put it all in one basket) it doesn't matter your present physical state-IT'S TIME TO RISE AND KNOW THAT YOUR ELEVATION BEGINS IN YOUR OWN MIND.

WHO ARE "THE FOLKS"

EACH PERSON THAT MAKES UP THE BLOCK IS A FATHER, MOTHER, DAUGHTER, SON, COUSIN, FRIEND OR HOMMIE OF SOMEBODY.

EACH PERSON IN THE BLOCK IS A HUMAN BEING WITH A SPIRIT. EACH PERSON IN THE BLOCK IS A PERSON WITH FEELINGS, HABITS, THOUGHTS, ACTIONS AND REACTIONS THAT ARE UNIQUE. EACH ONE OF US HAS A FUTURE THAT HAS BEEN DESIGNED BY HIS OR HER CREATOR! LORD GOD.

YEP! THAT'S RIGHT. EACH PERSON IN THE BLOCK IS A SPIRIT..EVEN YOU WHO HAVE DARED TO READ MORE.

IF YOU DIDN'T REALIZE THAT YOU ARE A SPIRIT HAVING A HUMAN EXPERIENCE; THEN, NOW YOU KNOW AND YOU WILL NEVER EVER BE THE SAME PERSON YOU WERE BEFORE. EVEN AT THIS POINT WHAT YOU LEARN IN READING "FOLK ON THE BLOCK RISE" IS TO BE SHARED AS YOU READ…LET GO…… OF ALL THAT YOU WERE TOLD ABOUT YOU.

DIRECT YOUR THOUGHTS

        TO WHAT YOU SEEK …FOCUS.

PULL WHAT YOU ARE SEEKING INTO THE PRESENT

        UNTIL IT SURROUNDS YOU…..THEN

PLAY IT FORWARD, WALK INTO IT

        SHARE IT WITH PEOPLE YOU TRUST.

The more we learn about ourselves. The easier it is to change

(6)*Pierre Teilhard de Chardin, a Christian, said. "Someday after we have mastered the winds, the waves, the tides, and gravity, we shall harness... the energies of love," he wrote. "Then for the second time in the history of the world, man will have discovered fire."

> When we learn that we are not perfect,
>> And learn to love ourselves in spite of our own imperfections
>>> Only then can we learn to love others in their imperfection.

The greatest teacher on loving the imperfect, undeserving, unlovable is LORD GOD as he has taught us through the teachings of Christ Jesus and imparted revelations to others.

DETERMINE WHO YOU ARE

WHICH boo(BOO) are you?

This might appear to be a really silly question; but before you make any conclusions about the inquiry...let's explore the word B00(boo)!

1. Boo – when said in a loud voice and in a manner in which the intended hearer does not know or is not aware of the origin of the sound. Is meant to scare the intended hearer.
2. Boo -is a 5-year-old Pomeranian with 1.5 million Facebook fans. The lovable pooch and his owner have put together the book, "Boo: The Life of the World's Cutest Dog

Now! I can add another "street" definition, thanks to my daughter Keisha: Boo- refers to a persons' SAD, DEFEATED perceptions of their life and is applied to a male or female..

Mr. or Ms. Boo. – a person who views their life as miserable, worthless, sad, without value.

Introduction

The purpose of this book is to assist individuals in identifying the higher person and highest level of living no matter your ethnicity, status or location or residence or age.

The reading is intended to be informative yet interesting and relative to the reader.

Why else would you be still reading? If we are not in a situation or perception that needs to be improved then you know someone who is in need of elevation.

These precepts from this master class for you are clear steps to move up in thoughts, spirit and life. Enjoy!

That which you seek *you already Are*

* Be careful what you call yourself…what you say returns to you fully developed

We are first Spirit. As the voice of God spoke us and everything into existence; the universe answered by obedience:

(5) Bible scriptures show us how God spoke first then there was manifestation for example in Ezekiel 43:2)"And, behold, the glory of the God of Israel came from the way of the east: and his voice was like a noise of many waters: and the earth shined with his glory"

We, the Folk in the Block put on a Human form and still are Spirits –(22) Psalm 139: 12 Even the darkness is not dark to You, And the night is as bright as the day. Darkness and light are alike to You. 13, For You formed my inward parts; You wove me in my mother's womb. 14 -I will give thanks to You, for I am fearfully and wonderfully made; Wonderful are Your works, And my soul knows it very well

Both spirit and body are connected to and formed by this same God, the creator, "I AM", Jehovah, Allah, Yahweh, JHVH, Elohim, …and we continue to be spiritual, Celestial beings having a desire to unite and connect with our Creator, the True Vine .(8) John 15:1 –"I am the true vine, and My Father is the vinedresser. 2"Every branch in Me that does not bear fruit, He takes away; and every branch that bears fruit, He prunes it so that it may bear more fruit.

The Spirit of Lord God has put in each of us a measure of Faith as stated in (9)Romans 12:3- "For by the grace given me I say to every one of you: Do not think of yourself more highly than you ought, but rather think of yourself with sober judgment, in accordance with the measure of faith God has given you"

(10) Hebrews 11:1, KJV Faith is substance of things hoped for, the evidence of things not seen . (11)Genesis gives us a great example of God declaring and afterward the manifestation appears

WHAT HAPPENS WHEN WE STEP INTO THE GREATER?

Then God said, "Let there be light"; and there was light (11) Genesis 1:3;
(12)2 Corinthians 1:4, "Let light shine out of darkness, the omnipotent, omnipresent spirit Lord God" made his light shine in our hearts to give us the light of the knowledge of God's glory displayed in {the face, physical actions, compassion} of Christ.

There is a process in transforming from being the basic Spirit in human form that walks and breaths on this earth to excelling into the Spirit in a human form whose actions (showing love, kindness, speaks life and light, expectations, creativity and healing..) Encompass the Greater. We can see the separation of the night sky from the day sky and the light in the stars shining-(12) Psalm 33:6 -By the word of the LORD the heavens were made; their starry host by the breath of his mouth.
(12) Psalm 33:9 For he spoke, and it came to be; he commanded, and it stood firm.

We learn to do as our father and Brother Christ Jesus..say it in faith and Expectation

Speaking the manifestation is provided as a template of understanding how God works you see with your eyes (the physical terrestrial realm) - (12)Psalm 33:6-9 "-By the word of the LORD were the heavens made; and all the host of ..." We are told that in the beginning was God.(10) Genesis 1: 14 -"And God said Let there be lights in the vault of the sky to separate the day from the night, and let them serve as signs to mark sacred times, and days and years" "(10)Genesis 1- 15 and" let them be lights in the vault of the sky to give light on the earth. And it was so". 16"God made two great lights—the greater light to govern the day and the lesser light to govern the night". He also made the stars. 17. "God set them in the vault of the sky to give light on the earth, 18. To govern the day and the night, and to separate light from darkness."

(10)Genesis 1:24 And God said, "Let the land produce living creatures according to their kinds:"
Even Greater did God expand territory – by speaking into existence and seeing the end in the present. (10) Gen: 1:26 Then God said, "Let us make ***mankind in our image***, in our likeness, so that they may rule over the fish in the sea and the birds in the sky, over the livestock and all the wild animals,[a] and over all the creatures that move along the ground."

THESE WERE THE FIRST FOLKS ON THE BLOCK— AND THEY WERE GIVEN TERRITORY TO RULE

God created mankind in his **OWN** image,

(10)in the image of God he created them;
>   male and female he created them.

28   God blessed them and said to them, "Be fruitful and increase in number; fill the earth and subdue it. Rule over the fish in the sea and the birds in the sky and over every living creature that moves on the ground."

29   Then God said, "I give you every seed-bearing plant on the face of the whole earth and every tree that has fruit with seed in it. They will be yours for food. 30 And to all the beasts of the earth and all the birds in the sky and all the creatures that move along the ground— everything that has the breath of life in it—I give every green plant for food." And it was so. Romans 8:16- The Spirit itself bears witness with our spirit, that we are the children of God:

What part of God in us is not Like God our Creator?

What substance of the ocean is not present when a part of it is put in a bottle? Is the same substance of a loaf of bread in a piece of bread?

So we who claim to be God's Children because we have the Spirit of God in us – the Holy Spirit- why aren't we speaking and manifesting, loving, being God, the Light for darkness.?

The answer is that we are not manifesting because we are not being enlightened to our purpose in the bible, God allowed mankind a choice to be one with him as he was one with Christ. Church Leaders have failed to teach "how each individual who believes in God can be one with God as spirits in the flesh", a spirits in human flesh and one with God.

God is Spirit and Word, then Word became Flesh (manifesting the invisible into visible) and dwelt among us..in the form of Jesus Christ, a spirit in human flesh and one with Father God. Those who allow the spirit of God to rule instead of our human emotions posses spiritual minds have enlightened us to the Mantra.

Mantra of becoming one with the spirits of God, who is Love.

The Greater Life is the promise and hope in the resurrection and union with the Spirit of God here on earth …until we "get It", the Folk on the block will be untouched by the five to ten churches in the Block where people are spiritually and physically dying. Look at the Block, several churches in a four block radius. What impact do they have on the lives of those who live on the Block? When we seek to do God's will , we have all the heavenly Gifts from God, why then teach dependence on religious routines that distract us from seeking of how to use our gifts.

(7)1 Corinthians 2:12:Now we have received, not the spirit of the world, but the spirit which is of God; that we might know the things that are freely given to us of God.

(13)1 John 4:2: Hereby know ye the Spirit of God: Every spirit that confessed that Jesus Christ is come in the flesh is of God (9)Romans 8:26: Likewise the Spirit also helped our infirmities: for we know not what we should pray for as we ought: but the Spirit itself maketh intercession for us with groaning's which cannot be uttered.

(12) Corinthians 12:13: for by one Spirit are we all baptized into one body, whether we be Jews or Gentiles, whether we be bond or free; and have been all made to drink into one spirit.

BUT NOT WITHOUT INSTRUCTION AND GUIDANCE

(8)John 1:1-In the beginning was the Word, and the Word was with God, and the Word was God. 2. He was in the beginning with God.

John 1:14-The Word became flesh and made his dwelling among us. We have seen his glory, the glory of the one and only Son, who came from the Father, full of grace and truth. (8)John 8:58 "Very truly I tell you," Jesus answered, "before Abraham was born, I am!" (speaking of the spirit within)

(8)John 17:5 And now, Father, glorify me in your presence with the glory I had with you before the world began

(14)Proverbs 8:23 I was formed long ages ago, at the very beginning, when the world came to be.

Just like our brother Christ Jesus, we were spirit formed when the world began and the Spirit of God has his presence in us to show his light yet show his glory through us

(22)Psalm 148:5 Let them praise the name of the LORD: for he commanded, and they were created.

God the Creator, the Great "I AM" has all that we need and all that we are and he put it in us to tap into the Greater by faith.

He gave us examples in Christ Jesus, John the Baptist, Disciples and those on whom the anointing (power of God) was given (Saul, David, Isaiah, Prophets of the old) to show us that being one with Father God gives us the ability to create, to dominate, to love, to Heal, to forgive, to have compassion, to be an example, to overlook all the actions of others that are contrary to God by using fruits of the Spirit of God in us (love, peace, forgiveness, not rushing to evil, respect) in our actions. In doing so we glorify our Creator, the Spirit of Divine Love from which we all originated and heal our families, communities and generations.

(15)Matthew 8:3 And Jesus put forth his hand, and touched him, saying,; I am willing," he said. "Be clean!" Immediately he was cleansed of his leprosy

(16)Ecclesiastes 7:8: Better is the end of a thing than the beginning thereof: and the patient in spirit is better than the proud in spirit.

(17)Numbers 11:25: And the LORD came down in a cloud, and spake unto him, and took of the spirit that was upon him, and gave it unto the seventy elders: and it came to pass, that, when the spirit rested upon them, they prophesied, and did not cease

(18)Malachi 2:15 And did not he make one? Yet had he the residue((19)DEFINED AS 1. something that remains after a part is removed, disposed of, or used; remainder; rest; remnant; material remaining after a distillation or an evaporation, or portion of a larger molecule In particular)of the spirit. And wherefore one? That he might seek a godly seed. Therefore take heed to your spirit, and let none deal treacherously against the wife of his youth. Even a part of a thing is the completely full of the whole of which it is a part.

(7) 1Corinthians 3:6 Who also - made us able ministers of the new testament; not of the letter, but of the spirit: for the letter killeth, but the spirit giveth life.

(20)Galatians 5:25: If we live in the Spirit, let us also walk in the Spirit

(21)Leviticus 11:44- For I am the LORD your God: ye shall therefore sanctify yourselves, and ye shall be holy; for I am holy: neither shall ye defile yourselves with any manner of creeping thing that creepeth upon the earth (emotions, thoughts)

(23)2 Peter 1:21- For the prophecy came not in old time by the will of man: but holy men of God spake as they were moved by the Holy Ghost.

(24)Jude 1:20:-But ye, beloved, building up yourselves on your most holy faith, praying in the Holy Ghost

(25)Exodus 30: 29-32" You shall consecrate them, that they may be most holy. Whatever touches them will become holy.

30- You shall anoint Aaron and his sons, and consecrate them, that they may serve me as priests. 31 And you shall say to the people......, 'This shall be my holy anointing oil throughout your generations. 32 It shall not be poured on the body of an ordinary person nor shall ye make any other like it, after the composition of it: it is holy, and it shall be holy unto you.

Given proper instructions using the free gifts, our oneness with God, our faith in his will in our lift, we impact those around us . there will be a GOD CHANGE on the Block.

DON'T BE LOYAL TO EVIL…NO MATTER WHAT

"DON'T KILL God's Plan for ME"

INSTRUCTION, OBEDIENCE THEN REWARDS.. FOR THE GREATER FOLKS IN THE BLOCKS, WE KNOW, IN SOME OF OUR BLOCKS TODAY THERE ARE FOLK WHO ARE NOT LOOKING OUT .. THEY ARE SUCKING IT ALL IN, TAKING THE LIFE OUT OF THE POSSIBILITIES THAT WERE PRESENT BACK IN THE DAY WHEN FOLKS ON THE BLOCK WERE LOVING, CONCERNED ABOUT EACH OTHER, WATCHED FOR THE SAFETY OF OUR YOUTH.

PRESENTLY, FOLKS IN THE BLOCK ARE RUDE, SPEAK OF DEATH AND DESTRUCTION. THEY HAVE NOT BEEN IMPACTED BY THOSE WHO CLAIM TO BE ONE WITH GOD. THE FREE GIFTS FROM GOD ARE NOT BEING USED TO ENLIGHTEN, GROW THE SPIRIT OF LIGHT, SHOW LOVE WHICH HONOR THE SPIRIT OF GOD IN US AS HUMAN BEINGS

WE HAVE HEARD THAT SATAN CAME TO A COUNCIL WHERE GOD WAS PRESENT AND WHEN ASKED WHERE HE HAD BEEN;

TRUTH CAME OUT-

Then Satan (deception, untruth, hatred)answered the LORD and said, "From roaming about on the earth and walking around on it. Seeking whom I may destroy. Darkness came to the light, doesn't mean there was no choice. " (13)1 John 3:8-10 ...The Son of God appeared for this purpose, that He might destroy the works of the devil, also known as: "the accuser,: "a traducer" (a slanderer, a false accuser)

The devil and Satan ARE one and the same entity and is also called "the tempter" (see(15) Matt 4:1-3 and vs.10, the evil one (15)(Matt 13:38). CHOOSE YOU THIS DAY WHO YOU WILL SERVE

AS FOR ME AND MY HOUSE WE SERVE THE TRUE AND LIVING GOD

(15)The Devil knows, uses and quotes Scriptures to promote false doctrine and deceptions (see Matt 4:1- 11).

He sends his people in the Kingdom (see (15)Matt 13:38-39).

He can take away the word of Gods from the heart of His people ((26) Luke 8:10-13). This is why we are to guard our hearts (what we allow ourselves to say, do and hear) with all diligence

He puts evil into the heart of men to betraying the Son(s) of God ((8)John 13:2).

Folks on the Block Rise

The Spirit that is opposed to the Spirit of Love (Satan) causes oppression / burdens to the point that healing is needed ((27)Acts 10:38-39).

If you let the sun go down on your anger you give the devil an opportunity ((28)Eph 4:25-28).

He schemes against us ((28)Eph 6:11-12).
He is able to hold people captive (29)(II Tim 2:25-26). He is like a roaring lion seeking someone to devour ((30)I Peter 5:8-9).

He has works (negative influence) ((13)I John 3:8-9).
He is capable of deceiving the whole world ((31)Rev 12:8-9). He can enter into the spirit of some people ((26)Luke 22:3-4). He can sift people like wheat ((26)Luke 22:31-33).

Satan – the Spirit opposed to the Spirit of God (Love)
- tries to use you to lie to the (Holy)Spirit of truth and love ((27)Acts 5:3), has a dominion of darkness (27)Acts 26:16-18). To combat him we use Gods word (in the flesh- actions of love, light, forgiveness and wisdom) to fight;

*Jesus used Scripture to fight him and then told him to be gone ((15)Matt 4:1-11).

*Satan falls (and his plan fails)when we use the authority & power given to us ((27)Luke 10:17-20).

- has schemes ((12)II Cor 2:10-11). He has angels ((33)Rev. 12:8-9).

- can be disguised as an angel of light ((12)II Cor 2:10-11).
-Can hinders us for a moment ((32)I Thes 2:17-19).
-Can exhibit False "Power", "Signs", & "Wonders" ((32) II Thes 2:9-10).

*Some are deceived and turn & follow Satan(evil) ((33)I Tim 5:14-16).
-has a synagogue, a throne ((31) Rev. 2;8-10,2;12-14.
OUR PURPOSE IN BEING ONE WITH GOD IS NOT FOCUESED ON WHAT EVIL DOES OR CAN DO; BUT ON WHAT LIGHT , ALBEIT, GIFT FROM GOD, WE CAN BRING INTO THE SITUATION

What I want to share

TIME TO MAKE IT PERSONAL

1. WHAT CAN YOU IMAGINE YOURSELF TO BE
2. ALIGN YOUR IMAGINED SELF WITH THE LOVE OF GOD
3. ADJUST YOUR IMAGINED SELF TO BE CONSISTENT WITH THE SOURCE OF YOUR SPIRIT - THE GOD OF LOVE.
4. LOOK TO THE LIFE AND TEACHINGS OF CHRIST AS A MODEL, EVEN THOUGH OTHERS LIKE GHANDI, SHARE TEACHINGS OF LOVE, CHRIST IS THE ONLY MODEL OF SPIRITUAL RESURRECTION AND ONENESS WITH GOD AFTER THE CONFINEMENT IN HUMANIT AS THE PROMISE OF ETERNITY.
5. WRITE YOUR MANTRA – HOW YOUR WILL ACHIEVE YOUR TRANSFORMATION
6. PRAY/ MEDITATE ON SCRIPTURE OR MANTRA REFERENCE
7. PUT A LOCK ON SHARING YOUR IMAGINED SELF UNTIL IT IS MANIFESTED

MY JOURNEY

I SPOKE OF GOING TO HAWAII A YEAR AGO; I SAW MYSELF THERE AND AS TIME PASSED AND I WENT ON SEVERAL TRIPS IN THE STATES THAT WERE CLOSE TO ILLINOIS OR JUST A COUPLE OF HOURS IN FLIGHT, AN ASSOCIATE MENTIONED TO ME THAT HAWAII WOULD BE A PLACE TO VISIT. I WAS EXCITED BUT HAD TO SEE IF I COULD FIND A PLACE TO STAY AND I SAW IN MY SPIRIT MIND MONEY TO TAKE THE TRIP.

I BEGAN WRITING THIS BOOK FROM HAWAII, KONA ISLAND. MY BROTHER'S TIME SHARE OPENED UP FOR THE EXACT WEEK I PLANNED TO GO; I BOOKED A FLIGHT FIRST CLASS (something everyone should enjoy at least once in life) . MY GOD SISTER, GAVE ME HER COUSIN'S NUMBER . WHEN I CALLED THE COUSIN, WHO LIVES IN HONLULU, SHE INVITED ME TO VISIT FOR A DAY. SHE OFFERED TO ACCOMMODATE ME AND TAKE ME TO ALL THE TOURIST SITES… ITS WAS ALL THERE; BUT INTENTIONS, FAITH AND CONNECTION TO GOD'S PLAN ALIGNED IT FOR MANIFESTATION.

Rev Attorney Dr. Theresa McCoy

THE BEGINNING OF THE YEAR I HAD EXPERIENCED MANY CHANGES (DIVORCE, MOM TRANSITIONED INTO THE SPIRIT, SINGLE PARENT OF TWO ADOPTED TEENS ….AND THOUGHT I WAS COMING TO RELAX; INSTEAD, I HAVE BEEN WRITING WITH THE INTENTION OF SHARING WHAT I HAVE LEARNED WITH THE FOLKS ON THE BLOCK..BECAUSE
I SEE OPPRESSION AND NEEDLESS DISPAIR THAT CAN ONLY BE REMOVED BY THE SPIRIT OF THOSE WHO OCCUPY THE BLOCK.

SHARING:

INSPIRED BY "I AM " ESSAYS WHICH I AUTHORED AND REGISTERED

WHEN I WAS A PRE-TEEN, I HAD BEEN MOLESTED AND DID NOT FEEL THAT LIFE AS I HAD EXPERIENCED IT , THUS FAR , WAS WORTH GOING FORWARD.

THIS WAS THE SAME YEAR MY AUNT, WHOM I WAS NAMED AFETER, DIED OF INFLUENZA. I HAD TO GO TO A DENTIST NEAR HER HOME BECAUSE OF A TRAUMATIC TOOTH EXTRACTION. DURING AN ALTERCATION WITH MY ELDEST BROTHER, HE KNOCKED OUT MY FRONT TEETH. I WAS TWELVE YEARS OLD AT THE TIME. BECAUSE OF THE FREQUENT VISITS TO THE DENTIST , I WAS AT MY AUNT THERESA'S HOME OFTEN.

ON ONE PARTICULAR VISIT SHE WAS ILL AND WHEN I ASKED IF I SHOULD CALL THE AMBULANCE, SHE REFUSED. WHITIN A WEEK MY DAD AND UNCLE CARRIED HER TO THE HOSPITAL. MY DAD VISITED MY AUNT DAILY. DURING ONE OF MY DAD'S VISITS TO THE HOSPITAL, I WAS AT HOME IN MY BEDROOM. MY BROTHER, TEYON WAS TEETHING AND FUSSY.

WHILE IN THE ROOM, I SAW THE FACE OF MY AUNT THERESA SHE

LOOKED ME IN MY FACE EYE TO EYE. HER NECK AND FACE WAS

SURROUNDED BY THE BRIGHTEST LIGHT I HAD EVER SEEN. I SAW HER

HAND COME OUT OF THE LIGHT AND TOUCH MY RIGHT KNEE.

I FELT ENERGY CIRCLE MY BODY FROM THE RIGHT KNEE UPWARD AND

AROUND AND THEN SHE DISAPPEARED. I GOT UP AND TOLD MY MOM

THAT AUNT THERESA WAS DEAD. SHE WANTED TO KNOW HOW I

KNEW AND I TOLD HER "I JUST SAW HER".

THE EXPERIENCE OF THAT ENERGY MADE ME CURIOUS AND

CHANGED MY PERCEPTION OF LIFE FROM NOT BEING WORTH LIVING TO A DIRECTION OF ASKING "I WONDER WHY" TO THIS OR THAT. I WENT ON TO

PLAY SPORTS IN MIDDLE SCHOOL AND HIGH SCHOOL WHILE STILL BEING

MOLESTED. AFTER GRADUATION I WAS PROMISED A CAR IF I STAYED HOME TO;

GO TO COLLEGE BUT MY MOM INFORMED ME THE FIRST SEMESTER THAT IT

WAS HER CAR SO I TRANSFERRED FROM PURDUE CALUMET TO HOWARD

UNIVERSITY – COLLEGE OF NURSING.

At Howard I met some wonderful people. The family of my best friend Monica(now deceased) of Prince Georges County embraced me as their own. My best friend Monica showed and shared love of family like I had never experienced.

While living in the quadrangle dormitory, Crandall Hall, I learned that the effects of being violated manifests in strange ways later in life. I was asked by my dormitory mates why I had cow bells on my dormitory room door. I didn't figure it out until later that I used it as a warning that someone was about to come into my bedroom.

I Received a Bachelor of Nursing from Howard University . During my senior year, I chose a project in community health. In researching this project my questions that I asked when my aunt passed about influenza and disease were answered.

Into my fifth year of practice as a Professional Registered nurse, I had no interest in changing professions until I stumbled onto a legal brief about negligence.

Years later I moved back to Indiana and while speaking with my dentist, the same dentist who cared for me when I visited my aunt, he inspired me to continue my education. I later was in an accident and used the negligence brief to win a settlement.

I used that money to go to Law school. My friend Monica opened her home for me to stay for the first semester . Can you see how the doors kept opening as I walked into Gods' destiny for my life.

It's not magic, I had to act, do something, not just sit there dreaming.

My dentist told me "apply to law school and don't tell them you aren't qualified, let them tell you" Well I applied, Got accepted and I did well. I was invited to write for the law journal after the first year while I worked full time night shift as a critical care nurse. The professors knew me as "The Nurse" . I interned at the Justice Department as a student Prosecutor in the felony division. By error I spent the first couple of weeks with a prosecutor who spent most of our time talking about basketball, His nephew was playing for a popular east coast school and one of my younger brothers played at the University of Maryland as their Point Guard. At one point this particular prosecutor asked me if African Americans were afraid of dogs. I was stunned and asked "why did you ask me that"? His response was that, the entire African American community is scared of dogs because of the use of dogs by various police during Freedom Marches. Let it sink in how ridiculous that sounded to me. I was later transferred to the proper prosecutor who gave me great advice and tips. There were other student prosecutors represented from Georgetown, George Washington and American, University ;but I was the only one from Howard University School of Law. I graduated in three years;that was in 1987.

My path was set, I just had to be in line, sober, open, intentional, willing and have faith.

I must add that for 13 years I struggled with faith and intentions as most do who have not allowed healing from childhood abuse....the plan was still waiting for me to get on board and rise.

I later met a man of God " Chief Apostle", who anointed me and opened a door to oversee the Midwest Bible College.I received a Masters in Theology and a Doctorate in Ministry and encourage the graduates to write and publish what the spirit has revealed to them...to say" it's already in you already have it, just bring it out"

SO YOU TOO CAN RISE...TO THE PLAN GOD HAS SET FOR YOUR..CONNECT WITH THE HOLY SPIRIT- THE SPIRIT OF GOD-WHO IS LOVE

(34)Proverbs 18:21 (KJV)21 Death and life are in the power of the tongue: and they that love it shall eat the fruit thereof

FOLK ON THE BLOCK MUST CREATE A BETTER FRUIT FOR THE GREATER AND ITS ALL IN THE TONGUE

Christians talk about the trinity, the triune of Father son and Holy Spirit I I heard that Hindus and Buddhist aspire to the inner light, consciousness.

Others just talk about getting connected to the one source of all who is God the creator

Mos spiritual leaders acknowledge that we begin with the unseen and our own state of mind.

Let's just explore the triune. We are so interconnected so interconnected with the triune, we should see miracles in our house of prayer as was seen in the days of Christ where the holy spirit was imparted upon certain people (apostles) through an anointing rather than being accepted as a free gift to all who are willing to connect. Look what happens when we are connected to the father as was Jesus- the triune is as a threefold cord that is not easily broken. (8)John 15:1"I am the true vine, and My Father is the vinedresser. 2Every branch in Me that does not bear fruit, He takes away; and every branch that bears fruit, He prunes it so that it may bear more fruit"

When we are truly connected to our creator ….WE USE THE GREATER IN EACH OF US TO TRANSFORM THE FOLK IN THE BLOCK. THAT IS OUR OWN INDIVIDUAL RESPONSIBILITY. EVERYONE AFFECTS EVERYBODY,

"TIME" IS HERE FOR THE BODY BUT THE SOUL IS ETERNAL. ETERNITY HAS NO PAST OR FUTURE, IT ALL EXISTS IN THE PRESENT- THE HERE AND NOW

THE CYCLE OF REAPING WHAT YOU SOW, OR YEN/YANG ARE REFLECTIONS OF WHAT HAPPENS IN TIME AND ETERNITY.

WHEN YOU DO GOOD OR BAD IT WILL RETURN TO YOU; BUT THE CONCEPT OF OPPOSITES KNOWS THAT IT IS ALL IN THE PRESENT IT EXISTS ALREADY

THE PROCESS OF
GREATER….TRY IT

(THIS IS YOUR TIME TO PRACTICE)
WE MUST PLACE IT IN OUR MIND,
ESPECIALLY RIGHT BEFORE WE SLEEP
OUR DREAMS OUR THOUGHTS
ALIGN IT WITH THE GOD OF CREATION – GOOD,
LOVE, ETERNITY, THINGS THAT ARE OF GOOD
REPORT, JOY AND SPEAK IT INTO THE PHYSICAL
EXISTENCE BY FAITH
SAY IT FEEL IT AS IF IT HAS HAPPENED
ANTICIPATE THE MANIFESTATION

(8)John 15:3"You are already clean because of the word which I have spoken to you.4"Abide in Me, and I in you. As the branch cannot bear fruit of itself unless it abides in the vine, so neither can you unless you abide in Me.5"I am the vine, you are the branches; he who abides in Me and I in him, he bears much fruit, for apart from Me you can do nothing.6"If anyone does not abide in Me, he is thrown away as a branch and dries up; and they gather them, and cast them into the fire and they are burned.7"If you abide in Me, and My words abide in you, ask whatever you wish, and it will be done for you.8"My Father is glorified by this, that you bear much fruit, and so prove to be My disciples.9"Just as the Father has loved Me, I have also loved you; abide in My love

10"If you keep My commandments, you will abide in My love; just as I have kept My Father's commandments and abide in His love.11"These things I have spoken to you so that My joy may be in you, and that your joy may be made full. Connection to the spirit of truth provides our spirit with knowledge of who we really are outside of our vessel (body). (8)John 15:29 26"When the Helper comes, whom I will send to you from the Father, that is the Spirit of truth who proceeds from the Father, He will testify about Me; 27-and you will testify also, because you have been with Me from the beginning " – the spirit of man comes from God and is always connected but blocked by human emotions, lack of faith, lack of intention to acknowledge the connection and ignorance.

"The spiritual Law of Giving and Receiving teaches us that in order to attract or receive something in our lives, we need to give it freely and without expectation. If we want to experience more love, we need to be lavish in our own expression of love. To receive acceptance, we need to be open and accept others. Today choose one quality that you want to expand in your experience and find as many opportunities as you can to share that same quality with others"-quoted from (7) Ophra.com in her 21 day challenge meditation

TO BE SHARED WITH ALL THE FOLKS ON THE BLOCK WHERE YOU LIVE, TEXT, PARTY, KIC, TWEET, EMAIL, INSTAGRAM. THE UNIVERSE IS WAITING.

IT BEGINS WITH YOU..BOO

POEMS

Are you
Living
The love in you
When you
Slap my emotions to
Boost your ego
Tell me I'm your queen
But are never seen
With your queen
Nor applaud her drive

LIVING THE LOVE INSIDE

In sink
In Peace
Overwhelming clarity
Is our living when we
Live the love inside
Are you
When you
Hear me without listening
Say! But do the opposite

Her again

Can you hug
Her when she feels pain
Do you
Should you dare
Live that love you've hid so well
Inside
Maybe then
We can share (@8/2000

Poems of inspiration

P.U.S.H.

To overcome adversity
Must one walk into it or
Invite it in our path
A fight with clinched fist
A single finger or flick of the wrist may be the catalyst
Even without the act of one
Adversity past gone will again come and come again with the same taste, similar furry and a different fact but die at will when we admits it's existence and in us it is resolved
@2001
"I am essays – Theresa McCoy

ESSENCE OF PRAYER

I ASK THE LORD to guide

my thoughts and actions as I Go
through those things
in life which
Tend to
Loosen and erode the physical
and spiritual
Connections that make
Up my being
My Faith moves with my
request as such
Peace is at hand
(8/30/2000

I'M HERE (Cause I stop getting High)

I am so blessed
Not to be there

Where? There Where is There?

A state of mind that is not here and now
If it's not here and now
then where would there
be?

There is somewhere else, where what
you do or think you do And what you
feel or think you feel

Is unreal in its effect
and perception;

Then, why go there?

To get out of here.

How do you get back here from there
Stop doing what you do to get
there.

FEEL

Tranquility surrounds my soul
Each day I awaken

Smell the air. See the variation of
colors before me.

In animals, plants and humans alike

Singing "I AM" when I hear chimes
from the breeze and smell grass being
cut or hear water splashes while
flowing downstream.

Happy and fulfilled
I stand before thee who created it all
Just from his spoken word.

GOIN TO CHURCH

Goin t'church!
what's that gonna do?

Hopefully inject God
in your point of
view ....So that
when evil come near
you will win, cause God is here in you

to show and correct too
the bad acts you
would ordinarily do
So when folks
provoke you
And do you harm

You can stay and pray ; or if you must walk away,
still pray in faith That God is there too.
That's what going t'church will do

The Spirit of the Devine is" the bomb"

I felt a loss of desire and a presence of God's spirits, pure and glorious. Satan is gone..I knew he would return again..and I will fight again and win because he is in me, The Spirit of the Devine is the bomb
Want a high that stays with you for days A thrill like no other
And it's free
No money, no crime
Just kneel or stand praying to the Lord. Take a hit, take a tote, and shoot it in your veins by letting the spirit of holiness in I know, I did it seven times a day I thanked him, acknowledged him and asked my God for a release of strength and wisdom ... then I prayed. And later I was stronger and added while on my knees "Satan I rebuke you by the power of Love and Truth given to me by Lord God, is what I said

CHOICES (@9/22/2000)

When you take that risk Thinking
no one will see
Know that God almighty is taking full view of thee Hoping
you seek to connect with him first Which gives him much
pleasure
His grace, love and blessings you share with those your see
everyday
Now is the time to show that in Jesus you are not ashamed
he will know your name among Gods and Angels

POSITIVE ENERGY

Living this life is more than merely an inhale
and exhale More than how a person appears
to himself or others More than a J.D or even a
Ph.D

Even more than living in wealth

Loving life is simply the appreciation one has for
all that lives The smallest creature or Planet
To the largest tree
The poorest child to the one who
lives in thee Being in the present,
feeling your energy Regenerating,
healing, creating
Just being
Loving life is more than the eye can see.

Loving

It is peace
It is harmony with earth, the universe
And all that is diverse
The Spirit and action are one
When you love life
You also love
The life
Looking back
At you.

STOPPING

It's never hard to stop
    No matter what it is
Gossip, lying
    Deceiving, crying,
        Buying, trying,
            Flying high, sexting,
                Texting, romancing,
                    Funky dancing
It's never hard
    But it's always
        A choice

BODY STUFF

We are the body of "I AM"

Talking about being an adoptive parent of the adolescent

What a hard Job. What need for God in pushing back the child you desired for the child that is.

Doesn't matter your plans! I saw and accepted it as an assignment. Found out there was plenty of scars. Hear a voice tell me that only God could heal those wounds, they were too deep. Just show them God's love and a mother's love, the small voice said. That was an easier task, I thought.

What I found was a journey of a deeper understanding of who I am. Who I am in God, as a person, as a Mother, In God. So the journey began.

FOLKS ON AMES STREET

DID THE ANNOINTING FALL ON AMES STREET – unedited version – (copyright 2010) Library of Congress – part of the "I AM" series Dr. Theresa McCoy

EARLY SATURDAY MORNINGS DURING MY MIDDLE SCHOOL AGE YEARS, I COULDN'T WAIT FOR 9:00AM. THAT WAS THE PROPER TIME IN WHICH YOU COULD CALL OR KNOCK ON A DOOR TO SEE IF THE OTHER KIDS ON THE BLOCK WERE UP. IT MIGHT HAVE JUST BEEN MY MOTHER, RUTH'S RULE, NONETHELESS.

IT'S 9:05am I RUN DOWN THE STREET, AMES STREET 900 BLOCK TO SEE IF MY BEST FRIEND WAS UP AND THEN MY PLAY SISTER SO THAT WE COULD PLAY DOUBLE DUTCH.

AMES WAS IN A PART OF HAMMOND, EAST OF THE TRACKS AND REFERRED TO AS EAST HAMMOND, ON AMES STREET THERE RESIDED THREE PASTORS (now deceased) OF THE GOSPEL MY DAD PASTOR BISHOP DR. ODESTRESS MCCOY IN THE NINE HUNDRED BLOCK AND an ELDER CHARLES TALIFERO IN THE TEN HUNDRED BLOCK AND CHARLES BURNS IN THE ELEVEN HUNDRED BLOCK. ALSO, ON AMES STREET FIVE RESIDENTS BECAME ATTORNEYS, EDUCATORS-PROFESSIONAL BALL PLAYER, IRVING CROSS,

PROFESSIONAL FOOTBALL PLAYER AND SPORTS ANNOUNCER, MUSICAL DIRECTOR OF HIT MOVIE SERIES (EMPIRE), ENTREPEUNERS (TWO OF WHICH ARE MY YOUNGERS BROTHERS), INSURANCE, INDIANA'S TOP THREE POINT SHOOTER, BUSINESSMEN, AND ACTOR- JAMES EDWARD WHO CHANGED THE STEROTYPE OF BLACK ACTORS (1) WIKIPEDIA -James Edwards (March 6, 1918 - January 4, 1970) was an African American actor in films and television. His most famous role was as Private Peter Moss in the 1949 film Home of the Brave, in which he portrayed a soldier experiencing racial prejudice while serving in the South Pacific during World War II. Other notable roles were in Stanley Kubrick's The Killing (1956) and John Frankenheimer's The Manchurian Candidate (1962). Edwards was prolific on TV in the 1960s, playing character roles in various series such as Peter Gunn, The Fugitive, Burke's Law, Dr. Kildare and Mannix, before his death of a heart attack at the age of 51. HIS NEICE still resides in East Hammond.

THE BORDERING STREETS ARE KENWOOD AND CONKEY DURING THE 1960'S, AMES WAS THE NEUTRAL PLACE FOR MORE THAN JUST DECIDING WHICH HIGH SCHOOL, MIDDLE SCHOOL AND GRADE SCHOOL YOU WOULD ATTEND BUT ALSO WHETHER YOU WERE CONSIDERED UPPER OR LOWER CLASS. THE BLOCK LOCATION OF AMES WAS ALSO OF SIGNIFICANCE.

KENWOOD WAS RELATIVELY QUIET; BUT MOST OF THE RESIDENCE ON THE 1000 CALLED TEN HUNDRED BLOCK AND ELEVEN HUNDRED BLOCK WERE STRUGGLING SOMEWHAT AND THERE SEEMED TO BE AN EXTRAORDINARY NUMBER OF FIGHTS, THE KIDS WERE CONSIDERED "BAD" BUT MOST HAD THE FAMILY UNIT INTACT. JUST ACROSS THE ALLEY FROM OUR HOUSE. THE YOUNG BOYS IN THE FAMILY WERE REFERRED TO AS "BAY BRO THEN" WOULD ALWAYS THROW ROCKS AT MY BROTHER RALAND. RALAND WAS ONE OF THE BEST PITCHERS IN THE NEIGHBORHOOD BASEBALL LEAGUE. I QUESS HE WAS BEING TESTED BY BAY BRO THEM TO SEE IF HE COULD THROW ROCKS AS WELL AS HE COULD A BASEBALL

ONE OF MY BEST FRIENDS LIVED IN THE ELEVEN HUNDRED BLOCK OF KENWOOD, SO I FREQUENTED THE AREA DAILY. HER AUNT WAS RAISED IN HER FAMILY LIKE SHE WAS HER SISTER, AND MY FRIEND GOT PREGNANT IN 9TH GRADE. I WONT MENTION HER NAME; BUT SHE HAS ALLOWED ME THROUGHOUT THE YEARS TO USE HER STORY. MANY THOUGHT, INCLUDING MY MOM, THAT SHE WOULD END UP NOT MAKING MUCH OF HER LIFE ; BUT SHE DID . I TAKE PLEASURE IN HAVING INTRODUCED HER TO ANOTHER FRIEND OF MINE WHOM I MET WHILE ATTENDING PURDUE CALUMET. THEY MARRIED AND HAVE FIVE CHILDREN,

BOTH ARE COLLEGE GRADUATES WITH ADVANCED DEGREES AND LIVE A VERY NICE, COMFORTABLE LIFE IN SOUTH BEND, INDIANA SO MUCH OF NAY SAYERS.

WHEN I WALKED ON KENWOOD, I WOULD CHANGE MY SWAGGER TO THAT OF BEING A LITTLE TOUGH. THAT WAY NO ONE WOULD TRY TO START A FIGHT; THE GIRLS FROM KENWOOD AND SOUTH OF KENWOOD SUCH AS MOSS STREET WERE KIND OF TOUGH..I THOUGH BACK THEN ANYWAY

THE STREET NORTH OF AMES WAS CONKEY; NOW WALKING DOWN CONKEY WAS NOT ONLY AN ADVENTURE ; BUT IT WAS ENLIGHTENING.

MY FAMILY

MY MOM WAS A BEAUTICIAN, SHE WENT TO ROBY'S BEAUTY COLLEGE IN GARY, INDIANA MY MOM WAS BORN AND LIVED IN GARY WITH MY GRANDPARENTS AND HER SIBLINGS. SHE CAME FROM A BIG FAMILY KNOWN AS THE BOZEMANS. MY GRANDPA, WILLIAM BOZEMAN ALWAYS TOOK TIME TO TELL US THAT WE WERE CHOCTAW INDIAN. HE WAS BORN IN JACKSON MISSISSISSIPPI, HAD WHITE SILKY HAIR AND A VERY PLEASANT PERSONALITY. MY GRANDMOTHER WAS FROM CHICAGO VIA TENNESSEE; SHE WAS SHORT, HAD THICH LONG HAIR AND PRAYED A LOT.

MY DAD WORKED AT INLAND STEEL COUNTING STEEL BARS. HE DIDN'T COMPLETE EIGHT GRADE. SELF TAUGHT IN ENGLISH. SPOKE ELEQUENTLY AND HAD GREAT HANDWRITING AND ABILITY TO EXPRESS HIMSELF IN WORDS AND SPEECH. HE WAS BORN IN TALLULA LOUISIANA WHERE HE SAID HE WOULD NEVER RETURN. SHARED HIS EXPERIENCE SEEING THE " STRANGE FRUITS" OF AFRICAN AMERICANS LYNCHED, TREATED INHUMANELY AND YOUNG AFRICAN AMERICANS SCARED FOR THEIR LIVES.

ONE OF HIS BROTHERS WAS SAID TO HAVE WITNESSED SOMETHING SO HORRIFIC HE LOST HIS SANITY.MY GRANDFATHER "POPS PETE" WAS A BLACKFOOT AND MY GRANDMOTHER MARIAH ROSBUD WAS A ROSBUD INDIAN AND FRENCH.

ANYHOW, MY MOM AND DAD WERE "SAVED" MEANING THAT THEIR BELIEF WAS APOSTOLIC REQUIRING THAT REPENTENCE AND ACCEPTANCE OF JESUS CHRIST AS SAVIOR AND LORD WOULD ASSURE SALVATION AND ETERNAL LIFE. I SHARED AND MINISTERED THE SAME.

WE HAD TWO MAJOR RULES AS A YOUNG LADY AND THAT RULE WAS WE WERE NOT TO BE SEEN ON CONKEY STREET AND WE ARE NOT TO BE THE ONLY GIRL IF THERE ARE MORE THAN TWO BOYS IN OUR PRESENCE. ALL OF MY MOTHER'S CLIENTS WERE TOLD THAT IF THEY SAW US ON CONKEY THEY HAD PERMISSION TO GRAB US OFF THE STREET AND BRING US HOME WHERE WE WOULD CERTAINLY GET A "WHOOPING",

THE BLOCK

IT WAS NECESSARY TO HAVE A REASON TO BE ON CONKEY STREET. CONKEY WAS THE BUSINESS AND PARTY DISTRICT.

IN THE LOW END OF THE TEN HUNDRED BLOCK WAS COLLINS CANDY STORE BUT NEAR THE ELEVEN HUNDRED BLOCK WAS THE CAVE, A NIGHT CLUB JOINT.

THE BROOKS HOUSE WAS THERE ON THE CORNER. THE BROOKS HOUSE WAS A COMMUNITY CENTER AND LIBRARY; IT HAD A WOODEN SKATING RINK ON THE SECOND FLOOR; A LIBRARY ON THE FIRST FLOOR AND ON THE SIDE OF THE BUILDING WAS A BASKETBALL COURT.

ON THE ELEVEN HUNDRED BLOCK WAS THE ABC FOOD STORE WHOSE SECURITY ALARM WOULD GO OFF AT LEAST ONCE A WEEK. AND THERE WERE VARIOUS LIQUOR STORES ON THE BLOCK AND, BARBEQUE CARRYOUTS, SHOOTINGS WERE NOT UNCOMMON AND FIGHTS AFTER HOURS AMONGS PATRONS OF" THE CAVE" WERE A SURE THING. MY FATHER'S SISTER, WAS STABBED IN THE NECK WHILE AT THE CAVE SITTING AT THE BAR. IT WAS A CASE OF MISTAKEN IDENTITY. MY AUNT LIVED; BUT DIDN'T FREQUENT THE PLACE ANYMORE. I THINK THAT S WHEN HER AND MY UNCLE DECIDED TO OPEN A SPEAK EASY IN THEIR BASEMENT. I DIDN'T KNOW WHAT THEY WERE DOING UNTIL I WAS OLDER; BUT MEN AND SOME WOMEN WOULD BE IN THE BASEMENT,

MUSIC PLAYING, MY AUNT WOULD COOK AND THEY MADE MONEY.

I LATER UNDERSTOOD THAT MY PATERNAL GRANDFATHER WAS A GRAND MASON, AND OWNED A CLUB; KEPT POLICY MONEY AND CARRIED A BIG RIFLE. MY DAD, A BISHOP, KEPT THAT SAME RIFLE BEHIND OUT FRONT DOOR. I NOW HAVE THE RIFLE.

I WAS NAMED AFTER ON OF MY FATHER'S SISTERS. FUNNY HOW PEOPLE CARRY ON A TRADITION.

BACK TO THE NEIGHBORHOOD . SINCE THE CANDY STORE WAS ON CONKEY, OWNED BY A NEIGHBORHOOD ENTREPRENEUR, THAT WAS A LIGITIMATE REASON TO BE ON CONKEY; THEREFORE WE WERE TOLD THAT" IF WERE SEEN PAST COLLINS CANDY STORE DON'T BE SURPRISED IS ONE OF MAMA'S CLIENTS GRABS YOUR BUTT UP AND BRING YOU HOME TO GET IT." ON OCCASION WE HAD TO GO TO THE FOOD STORE; BUT NEVER BEFORE DARK.
MANY EVENINGS DURING THE WEEK AND ALWAYS ON WEEKENDS, OUR NEIGHBOR, WOULD STUMBLE FROM CONKEY STREET TO HER HOME SEVERAL HOUSES AWAY FROM OUR HOUSE. WE LIVED ON THE CORNER, SO WE COULD SEE A LOT, ESPECIALLY WHAT WAS HAPPENING ON CONKEY. SOMETIMES LAYING ON THE CURB IN A DRUNKEN STUPOR, SOMEBODY FROM THE

NEIGHBORHOOD WOULD HELP HER UP AND GET HER TO HER FRONT STEPS OR KNOCK ON HER DOOR. SHE WAS BEAUTIFUL, HAD LONG HAIR, DARK BROWN SKIN; IN HER LATER DRUNKEN YEARS SHE BEGAN TO LOOK FRAGILE AND HAD MANY SCARS FROM HER FALLS

I SPENT PLENTY OF TIME SLOWLY WALKING DOWN CONKEY TO THE LIBRARY. THE LIBRARIAN AT BROOKS HOUSE FOUND THAT I LIKED TO READ, AND EVERY WEEK SHE WOULD HAVE A NEW BOOK, A MYSTERY FOR ME TO READ. I READ KING ARTHER BOOKS, MYSTERYS, AND FUNNY BOOKS. ONE DAY, I DECIDED TO PICK A REALLY BIG BOOK I CHOSE THE AUTOBIOGRAPHY OF ANNE MOODY. AFTER READING THAT BOOK, I REALIZED I DID NOT WANT TO LIVE MY LIFE LIKE HER. IT WAS A PIVOTAL BOOK IN MY LIFE. TO THIS DAY WHEN I SEE THE LIBRARIAN AND THANK HER; I TELL HER SHE CHANGED MY LIFE AND IS ONE OF THOSE WHOM I CREDIT FOR MY THIRST FOR EDUCATION AND FOR MY CAREER AS AN ATTORNEY, MINISTER, THEOLOGIAN, LIFE COACH AND REGISTERED NURSE.

NOW AMES STREET COMPARED TO KENWOOD AND CONKEY WAS A SAFE PLACE TO LIVE NO MATTER WHAT BLOCK YOU LIVED IN.
ON THE EIGHT HUNDRED BLOCK OF AMES WAS WHAT WE CALLED A SAND BOTTOM. ACTUALLY THERE WAS A BRICK YARD COMPANY AND THE

Folks on the Block Rise

DUST TOOK UP MOST OF THE SOUTHERN PART OF THE BLOCK. MANY OF US HAD BRICK BARBEQUE GRILLS…HAND MADE..BECAUSE WE WERE ALLOWED TO GET DEFECTIVE BRICKS PLACE ON THE SIDE OF THE YARD BY WORKERS. ACROSS FROM THE BRICK YARD WAS AN AREA MORE ON KENWOOD BUT MOST OF US ON AMES WOULD PLAY HID AND SEEK THERE. IT REMAINS A WOODED AREA GROOMED BY THE MOORES WHO LIVE NEAR IT. I RECEIVED MY DEEPEST SKIN WOUNDS TRYING TO HIDE IN BUSHES WHERE GLASS AND SHARP OBJECT WERE THROWN.

THE ELEVEN HUNDRED BLOCK OF AMES WAS WERE TRINITY HALL WAS LOCATED . TRINITY WAS A BUILDING THAT HAD APARTMENTS AND A HALL THAT WAS USED BY THE COMMUNITY. I TOOK ETIQUETTE CLASSES AT TRINITY AND GIRL SCOUT MEETING WERE HELD THERE ALSO.

A BIRACIAL(THAT TERM WASN'T USED BACK THEN) COUPLE LIVED ON THE ELEVEN HUNDRED BLOCK, THEY HAD THREE OF THEIR OWN AND TWO OF OTHER FAMILY MEMBERS. I REALIZE NOW THAT THERE WERE SEVERAL FAMILIES ON AMES THAT RAISED CHILDREN OF THE PARENT'S SIBLINGS OR HAD TWO FAMILIES IN THE SAME DWELLING. SO MUCH LOVE AND SACRIFICE.

MY DAD'S YOUNGEST SISTER, LIVED WITH US FOR A WHILE, AFTER MOVING OUT OF OUR BASEMENT MOVED TO AN APARTMENT IN TRINIY HALL

THE TEN HUNDRED BLOCK OF AMES ALSO HAD APARTMENT BUILDINGS ON THE CORNERS ACROSS FROM TRINITY HALL.

ANOTHER FAMILY WHO LIVED IN THE MIDDLE OF THE BLOCK AND HAD A CHURCH CALLED EMANUAL TEMPLE ACROSS THE STREET. THE PASTOR'S WIFE STUDIED AT A BEAUTY SCHOOL IN JOLIET AND WAS TAUGHT BY MADAME C. J . WALKER...HER DAUGHTER, IS MY GOD SISTER AND FRIEND AND HER DAD WAS THE DISTRICT ELDER FOR THE STATE OF INDIANA'S PENTACOSTAL ASSEMBLEY OF THE WORLD –PAW

ON THE TEN HUNDRED BLOCK = A MASTER TEACHER, RETIRED ASSISTANCT PRINCIPAL, A SUCCESSFUL INSURANCE AGENT WHOSE DAUGHER IS A PROFESSIONAL MUSICIAN AND APPEARS WITH SINGERS LIKE BILLY JOEL AND JOHN MELENCAMP.

ON THE CORNER CLOSEST TO MY HOUSE WERE THE A WHITE FAMILY WHO RENTED OUT A GARAGE AS A HOME TO ANOTHER SMALL WHITE FAMILY WITH A YOUNG GIRL AND BOY. I REMEMBER ON NIGHT WE HAD COME HOME FROM CHURCH AND MY BROTHER RALAND...

Folks on the Block Rise

WHO ALWAYS NOTICES THINGS. SAID IT LOOK LIKE

SOME LIGHT IN THAT GARAGE HOUSE...TURNS OUT THERE WAS A FIRE...WE TOOK BLANKETS OVER THERE KNOCKED ON THE DOOR...THE WOMAN DIED... THE YOUNG GIRL WE WERE TOLD DID SURVIVE... LATER THEY ALL MOVED AND A FAMILY WITH TWINS MOVED INTO THE BASEMENT OF THE BIG HOME.

THE NINE HUNDRED BLOCK OF AMES ACROSS FROM MY HOUSE WAS A YOUNG FAMILY. THEIR MOTHER WAS VERY MUCH BOTHERED, THEIR DAD REALLY LOVED THEM; BUT IT APPEARED THAT THINGS DID NOT WORK OUT ; SO HE RAISE THE BOYS AND SHE LEFT WITH THE GIRL. ON OUR BLOCK WE ALL PLAYED TOGETHER, THERE WERE BOX CAR RACES, RUNNING ACROSS THE SPRINKLER, SITTING ON STEPS, DOUBLE DUTCH CONTESTS, CHALK GAMES, BASEBALL, FOOTBALL, BASKETBALL HOOPS, FRUIT TREES IN THE YARDS AND EVERYBODY ON OUR BLOCK WENT TO CHURCH. SO MUCH FUN AND SO MANY MEMORIES.

I REMEMBER THE POLISH FAMILY (there was an empty lot between us) NEXT DOOR. THEIR GRANDMOTHER WOULD MAKE THE BEST BREAD, YOU COULD SMELL IT THROUGHOUT THE BLOCK SHE WOULD YELL DOWN TO US

"TELL YOU MAMA TO COME GET SOME OF THIS BREAD" MY MOM WOULD SEND HER GREENS.

ANOTHER FAMILY THAT STAYED IN THE MIDDLE OF THE BLOCK, ALL OF THEM WERE TALL, EVEN THE GIRLS. MY FRIENDS WERE MAGGI AND ROSIE ESPECIALLY ROSE…WE WOULD WALK AND TALK AND TELL SECRETS..SOME SECRETS WERE SO SECRET I COULDN'T REMEMBER THEM.

ON AMES STREET WAS THE FIRST BLACK EDUCATION IN THE HAMMOND SCHOOL SYSTEM. IN HER ATTEMPTS TO OBTAIN EMPLOYMENT WITH THE SCHOOL CITY OF HAMMOND, MY GODSISTER RECALLS THAT THE SUPERINTENDENT OF THE SCHOOL CITY OF HAMMOND VOWED THAT HE WOULD NEVER HIRE AN AFRICAN AMERICAN (HE USED A DIFFERENT REFERENCE) TEACHER. ONE MONTH AFTER MAKING THAT STATEMENT, THE SUPERINTENDENT DIED AND ANNIE TAUGHT FIRST OR SECOND GRADE

UNTIL HER RETIREMENT AT MAYWOOD ELEMENTARY SCHOOL. I RECALL MANY OF MY FRIEND WERE VERY EXCITED TO HAVE MS. HICKS AS THEIR TEACHER.

IT TAKES A VILLAGE OF AMES

THE MORROWS WERE MY SECOND FAMILY. HE ONLY DAUGHTER, REBA, IS MY LITTLE SISTER.

AND HER BROTHER, WHOM I LOVE AS A BROTHE, JEFF MORROW IS A WELL ESTABLISHED JINGLES PRODUCER AND MUSICIAN, NOW MUSICAL DIRECTOR FOR THE HIT SERIES "EMPIRE". YOU HAVE HEARD MANY OF HIS JINGLES DURING COMMERCIALS. AS A CHILD, IF I WERE NOT AT HOME, MOST LIKELY I WAS AT THEIR HOME. CLOTE WAS A GRADUATE OF ONE OF THE HUBC SCHOOLS..FISK I BELIEVE..SHE TAUGHT ME HOW TO CROCHT AND ETIQUETTE.

ONE OF THE FAMILIES ACROSS THE STREET HAD FOUR BOYS. I DARED ONE OF THE BOYS.. TO CUT ME WITH A KNIFE…AN HE DID..I CARRY THAT SCAR ON MY HAND AND REMIND HIM OF IT ON EVERY OPPORTUNITY I HAVE., THE OLDEST BROTHER IS A MOST EXCELLENT CRIMINAL ATTORNEY, HIS SISTER WAS GROOMED TO BE A PARALEGAL WHILE WORKING WITH HER BROTHER IN HIS FIRM.

THEN THERE WAS THE HARPERS…. MY FRIEND IN THAT FAMILY WAS LYNN, SHE HAD A OLDER SISTER TINA WHO WAS THE FIRST ON OUR BLOCK TO BECOME A LAWYER . LAMONT, A COUSIN OF THE HARPERS LIVED ON THE NORTH SIDE OF THE STREET IN THE NINE HUNDRED BLOCK. LAMONT IS A CHILD PRODIGY, HIS MUSICAL TALENT IS WELL KNOWN IN THE AREA AS A PIANIST.

THE MY "OTHER MOM" ALSO LIVED NEXT TO MY FRIEND IN THE MIDDLE OF THE NINE HUNDRED BLOCK OF AMES STREET. THEY WERE ALSO LIKE FAMILY ..THEY LIVED NEXT TO MY PARENTS WHEN MY PARENTS LIVED ON FIELDS STREET..A STREET BEHIND CONKEY…MY OTHER MOM SWEARS THAT MY MOM ALMOST GAVE ME TO HER…MY MOM SAYS THAT SHE LET HER KEEP ME SINCE THEY DIDN'T HAVE ANY CHILDREN …HER AND MY DAD WENT TO MY GRANDAD PETE'S FUNERAL IN TALULAH LOUISIANA. MY MOM SAID I CRIED A LOT, SHE NEEDED A REST. I QUESS IT WAS EASY SINCE I WAS THE ONLY SIBLING NOT BREAST FED. I FIGURE THE BOND WAS NOT AS STRONG AND THAT THE MILK I REQURIED WAS EXPENSIVE.

SHE TELLS ME SHE ENJOYED ME AND POTTY TRAINED ME. HER AND HER HUSBAND JUST THINK OF ME AS THEIR GIRL. I LOVE THEM AND THEIR TWO CHILDREN.
WHAT WAS SO SPECIAL ABOUT AMES THAT I ASK IF THE ANNOINTING FELL ON AMES STREET….
WELLLLLLLLLLL

ON AMES STREET (3 BLOCKS) FIVE ARE ATTORNEY, NUMEROUS LANDLORDS AND ENTREPRENEURS, ACTORS, PRO SPORTS ANNOUNCER/PLAYERS/MARKETING AGENTS, TWO REGISTERED NURSES, FIVE MINISTERS, WERE NURTURED BY THE VILLAGE.

THERE WAS SO MUCH TALENT AND GROWTH WITHIN A THREE BLOCK RADIUS THAT GOD HAS TO GET THE GLORY..AND FOR MY LIFE…
I HAVE SURVIVED PHYSICAL ABUSE, MOLESTATION, ADDICTION,

STILL GOD BLESSED ME WITH ABILITY TO GRADUATE FROM HOWARD UNIVERSITY AND RECEIVED A BSN, DEANS AWARD AND LEADERSHIP AWARD AND LATER DOCTORATE IN JURISPRUDENCE, LAW JOURNAL INVITEE
MOST RECENTLY A MASTORS IN THEOLOGY AND DOCTORATE IN MINISTRY, ADMITTED TO PRACTICE LAW IN THE STATE OF ILLINOS, ILLINOIS DISTRICT COURT AND THE UNITED STATES SUPREME COURT AS WELL AS BEING LICENSED AS A PROFESSIONAL BSN NURSE, LEGAL NURSE CONSULTANT., PAST PRESIDENT OF SOUTH SUBURBAN NAACP, STANDFORD WHOS WHO RECIPIENT, ONE OF A FEW AFRICAN/NATIVE AMERICAN NURSE-ATTORNEYS..AND SO MANY OTHER BLESSINGS.
AMES STREET WAS NO PLACE SPECIAL.

IT WAS IN THE MIDDLE OF EVERY OPPPORTUNITY WHERE A KID COULD GET LOST IN FOOLISHNESS…….BUT.

FOR MANY OF US…THE ANNOINTING FELL ON AMES STREET

Rev Attorney Dr. Theresa McCoy

IF YOU LOOK FOR THE DEVIL YOU WILL FIND HIM EVERYWHERE

IF YOU LOOK FOR GOD YOU WILL FIND HIM ANY WHERE..HE IS IN YOU

Our community needs post traumatic and present day trauma healing

Do it for your family and your Community…..here is one Gift God gave me to assist our youth in sharing traumas, concerns and questions about life while teaching them to heal and be who they are meant to be.

TEA TIME

T- TIME

E- ETIQUETTE

A- APPLICATION OF GODS WORD IN OUR LIFE

T- TOGETHER

I- INFORMATION

M- MINISTERING TO THE SPIRIT

E- EXPECTATIONS OF SELF, OTHERS AND SOCIETY

SEVEN MONTHS, SEVEN MEALS, SEVEN TOPICS, SEVEN SATURDAYS

TEA-COOKIES　　　　　　SIPPING, TASTING VS GOBBLING AND DRINKING

SANDWICH AND TEA　　　CUTTING UP THE SANDWICH, SMALL BITES, CHEWING

SALAD, SETTINGS AND TEA　　WHICH FORK, CUTTING UP THE SALAD, BITS

SOUP AND MEAT (CHICKEN)　　CUTTING UP THE MEAT, BITE SIZE, SIPPING SOUP, THE NAPKIN

MEAT AND VEGETABLES　　PRACTICE OF CUTTING AND EATING, NAPKINS AND SOCIAL CONVERSATION

DESERTS　　　　　　HOW TO ORDER/EAT, SOCIAL CONVERSATION

THE FULL MONTY=LETS GO OUT AND EAT

SPIRITUAL LESSONS

WHAT DOES GOD WANT FROM HIS CHILDREN
R/T PARENTS
WHO IS THE BOSS
IMPORTANCE OF OBEDIENCE
WHO IS OVER THE PARENTS

HOW DO WE CHANGE WHAT HAS ALREADY HAPPENED

CONFESSION
REMEMBERING GRACE
KNOWING WHO GOD IS- OMNIPOTENCE, RAFI, GIRA, NICI
FAITH

WHAT ABOUT FEAR AND THE FUTURE

GODS PLAN IS SUPREME
WE CAN CHOOSE TO BE USED/PART OF THE PLAN
OUR FUTURE HAS NOTHING TO DO WITH WHAT WITH WHAT WE SEE CHOOSING LIFE IN CHRIST

FORGIVENESS

ENEMIES
FRIENDS WHO HURT US
FAMILY MEMBERS WHO HURT US
SCHOOL, ADULTS AND OTHERS
WHY IS FORGIVENESS IMPORTANT
WHO BENEFITS THE MOST

THE TEMPLE OF THE HOLY SPIRIT— PART I
RISKY BEHAVIOR
WHY IS IT CALLED RISKY
WHAT IS THE DANGER - TO HEALTH, LIFE, REPUTATION, FUTURE,
GUILT

DISEASES - SKIN (TATTOOS/ PIERCING), SEXUAL, CONTAGIOUS
LAP DANCING AND ATTIRE
THE TEMPLE OF GOD

OPEN FORUM

RELIGION, SHARING YOUR FAITH, THE BAIT (YOUR LIFE) IN HELPING OTHERS SEE THE LOVE OF THE ALMIGHTY

INFORMATION

ATTITUDE- RIGHT VS KIND

THE WINNER

BEING A FRIEND - TO A FRIEND/TO AN ENEMY

ATTENDING CHURCH- WHY? WHAT IS BEING FED- OBLIGATION TO READ THE WORD

WHAT DOES IT MEAN TO BE SAVED AND WHO IS THE HOLY GHOST

WALKING WITH GOD AND WALKING BY YOURSELF

OPEN FORUM / TESTIMONIES

FIRST SESSION

TEA-COOKIES   SIPPING, TASTING VS GOBBLING AND DRINKING SOCIAL CONVERSATION

WHAT DOES GOD WANT FROM HIS CHILDREN (Ephesians 6:1-6,
R/T PARENTS(Ephesians 6:2-3, Exodus 21:15,17)
WHO IS THE BOSS(Ephesians 6:1)(Proverbs 1:8)
IMPORTANCE OF OBEDIENCE(Proverbs 10:1,17:21, 19:13,26)
WHO IS OVER THE PARENTS (Proverbs 1:8, 3:1,4:1-4)

ATTITUDE- RIGHT VS KIND

SECOND SESSION

SANDWICH AND TEA   CUTTING UP THE SANDWICH, SMALL BITES, CHEWING

HOW DO WE CHANGE WHAT HAS ALREADY HAPPENED

CONFESSION
REMEMBERING GRACE
KNOWING WHO GOD IS- OMNIPOTENCE, RAFI, GIRA, NICI FAITH

THE WINNER - INTELLECTUALLY, EMOTIONALLY, PHYSICALLY, SPIRITUALLY

THIRD SESSION

SALAD, SETTINGS AND TEA WHICH FORK, CUTTING UP THE SALAD, BITS

WHAT ABOUT FEAR AND THE FUTURE

GODS PLAN IS SUPREME
WE CAN CHOOSE TO BE USED/PART OF THE PLAN
OUR FUTURE HAS NOTHING TO DO WITH WHAT WITH WHAT WE SEE
CHOOSING LIFE IN CHRIST

BEING A FRIEND - TO A FRIEND/TO AN ENEMY

FOURTH SESSION

SOUP AND MEAT (CHICKEN)   CUTTING UP THE MEAT, BITE SIZE, SIPPING SOUP, THE NAPKIN

FORGIVENESS

ENEMIES
FRIENDS WHO HURT US
FAMILY MEMBERS WHO HURT US
SCHOOL, ADULTS AND OTHERS
WHY IS FORGIVENESS IMPORTANT
WHO BENEFITS THE MOST

ATTENDING CHURCH- WHY? WHAT IS BEING FED- OBLIGATION TO READ THE WORD

FIFTH SESSION

MEAT AND VEGETABLES PRACTICE OF CUTTING AND EATING, NAPKINS AND SOCIAL CONVERSATION

WHAT DOES IT MEAN TO BE SAVED AND WHO IS THE HOLY GHOST
Ephesians 2:21, 1 Pet. 2:9
THE TEMPLE OF THE HOLY SPIRIT— PART I

RISKY BEHAVIOR
WHY IS IT CALLED RISKY
WHAT IS THE DANGER - TO HEALTH, LIFE, REPUTATION, FUTURE,

GUILT (ABORTION, REPUTATION)

SIXTH SESSION

DESSERTS — HOW TO ORDER/EAT, SOCIAL CONVERSATION

THE TEMPLE OF THE HOLY SPIRIT— PART II
DISEASES - SKIN (TATTOOS/ PIERCING), SEXUAL, CONTAGIOUS
LAP DANCING AND ATTIRE
THE TEMPLE OF GOD

SEVENTH SESSION

THE FULL MONTY=LETS GO OUT AND EAT

WALKING WITH GOD AND WALKING BY YOURSELF
OPEN FORUM / TESTIMONIES

RELIGION, SHARING YOUR FAITH,

BEING FISHER'S OF MEN - THE BAIT (YOUR LIFE) IN HELPING OTHERS SEE THE LOVE OF THE ALMIGHTY (HOLLA)

PRELUDE

THE PURPOSE OF GOD'S INSPIRATION TO ME FOR WRITING THIS OUTLINE FOR COMPLETENESS DURING ADOLESCENCE IS THAT HE WILL BE GLORIFIED AND KNOWN TO THE YOUNG LADIES IN THIS MILLENNIUM AS A CATALYST IN CHANGING THE MANNER OF BEHAVIOR IN THE MALE AND FEMALE YOUTH THAT THEY MAY SEEK HIM IN THEIR TRANSITION TO MATURE ADULTS AND CHRISTIANS.

MY VISION

THAT THESE YOUNG GIRLS KNOW THE GOD ALMIGHTY AND THE FEAR OF HIS JUDGMENT CREATE OBEDIENCE, AND REFERENCE TO HIS GUIDANCE IN OUR LIFE AS WE OBTAIN

UNDERSTANDING AND THAT THE KNOWLEDGE OF THE GREAT PLANS HE HAS FOR THEIR LIFE AND HIS LOVE FOR US STRENGTHEN THEM AS THEY TRANSITION THROUGH DISAPPOINTMENT, HURT, AND PAIN THAT WE HAVE ALL EXPERIENCE IN OUR YOUTH. ESPECIALLY THOSE WHO HAVE EXPERIENCED RAPE AND MOLESTATION THAT THEY KNOWING THE FORGIVENESS THAT GOD HAS SHOW US AND MANKIND WHILE WE DID NOT DESERVE HIS GRACE, SHOW AND BE ABLE TO FORGIVE THOSE WHO VIOLATE THEM..AND FORGIVE THEMSELVES..LET GO OF GUILT SO THAT IT DOES NOT CHOKE AND STRANGLE YOUR GOALS AND HAPPINESS AS I EXPERIENCE SUCH BONDAGE FOR OVER THIRTY YEARS BEFORE I WAS ABLE TO LAY IN GOD'S GRACE AND MERCY AND PEACE

APPLICATION

ADAPT THE SESSIONS TO THE GIRLS IN YOUR PARTICULAR GROUP KNOWING YOU ARE STEWARDS ...BEING PRAYERFUL AT THE BEGINNING OF EACH SESSION, DURING EACH SESSION AND IN ENDING EACH SESSION FOR EACH CHILD AND THE PARENT .

Author/registered with Library of Congress 2006 from Lord God to Rev. Dr. Theresa McCoy

STAY AWAKE - you hold the key in getting quality healthcare

In order to fulfil any of our assignments we must know the rules in the arena we are placed…..at the present time we are in a preventive healthcare setting. When we don't know the rules…you know the rest…you get the "okie doke.." I went to the "21st Century healthcare for health professionals at the National Academy of Science in 2001… that was the inspiration for the following. IT IS CALLED LUNCINDA'S 21ST CENTURY HEALTHCARE
LUCINDA IS AWAKEN IN THE MIDDLE OF THE NIGHT WITH A SHARP PAIN ON IN HER UPPER LEG AND IS FEELING DIZZY

LUCINDA turns on the light above her bed. She turns on her iphone, goes to the internet and begins to access her medical record.
She types the symptoms she is experiencing. Many of Illnesses have the same symptoms ;but her medical doctor and team know her history and medication.

She is not able to speak so she turns on the palm pilot and types in her medical identification number; symptoms experiencing are listed on the internet connected to her medical provider team screen. She then clicks the symptoms and types in those that are not listed . Next, Lucinda clicks the shapely yellow button, which signals her iphone, electronic medical device or computer to call her healthcare team immediately and alert them that she is having serious symptoms. The team responded changed her prescriptions, sent a Nurse Case Manager to her home and ordered labs at a location of Lucinda's choice.

Being able to describe her symptoms was not always an easy task. Years ago, Lucinda learned to write down everything she felt before ..,.visits to the doctors. She attended a training seminar, which gave her confidence and information on her rights as a patient. She learned to give and receive information about herself and her Problems

2 Six months ago, while Lucinda was a hospital patient. She was introduced to several people who wanted a relationship with her during her healing process. These people worked as a team. They discussed with Lucinda her health problems and her understanding of her diagnosis and symptoms. The team was responsible for designing a plan of care with Lucinda and her family members in making choices available for her treatments. She was provided with information about available medications and side effects of each medication and treatment

FOR DOCTOR VISITS. She realized that she should always have a list of medications she is taking which includes vitamins and over the counter as well as prescription medication; have a family member or friend accompany her and listen or write down doctors instruction after the office visit it.......staff. at the doctor's office or hospital should explain what she was expected to do before the next office visit.

Ask questions about medication

Lucinda was asked if she had any questions. Lucinda had researched new medications and side effects, spoke with a pharmacist about alternative medication, and researched any new signs or symptoms before her doctors appointment. For this appointment, Lucinda had no questions.

LUClNDA's   friends-2 Rosita and D'bra

Lucinda friend. Rosella IS a MEDICAL herbal QUEEN. SHE asks questions but does not follow directions. Rosita adds her own prescribed dosage without sharing this information with the healthcare team She uses e-mail to communicate with a healthcare ·team she receives information emailed from team, the failure of Rosella ability to receive quality healthcare is that she fails to share with the healthcare team that she uses other supplemental herbal remedies and doesn't realize that herbs affects medication effectiveness and the quality of care Rosita receives.

In the 21st century healthcare system

The patient will call the shots. Even if the doctor disagrees, if there is a evidence supporting the medication or treatment, the patient has a choice.

There is mutual participation with science and ...evidence based; plan offered. The patient discusses her concerns with the team and if all are in agreement of the plan and or optional plans will then that's how it will proceed.

Lucinda's friend, D'bra must use the telephone to communicate with health provider. She hasn't purchased a computer although she is computer literate. This makes

D'bra more reliant on face-to face doctor visits and the four (4) hour wait to you see the doctor.

She spends an average of 10 minutes with her physician. The Office staff provides her with verbal Instructions regarding home treatment or medication. She doesn't have access to any of her records and neither does any other physician her regular doctor may refer her to for a consultation.

D'bra is ten years younger than Lucinda. She has insurance.

The new system is available to her; but she doesn't get checkups. She doesn't even question her doctor about new treatments or medications because he is an old friend.

Lucincda speaks with D'bra about how to get better healthcare service by participating in the decisions about her treatment; but there is no change . Of course, D'bra continues to complain about her service, nurses not giving her information or the right instructions. Her problems will continue until she, is more active in her healthcare decision and prevention.

REFERENCE

1. www.dictionary.com/browse/residue
2. Webster Dictionary's Definition of BLOCK
3. Micah 4:13, KJV Life in the Spirit Study Bible, copyright 1993,2005 by life publishers International
4. Tara Brach, a psychologist and instructor of mindfulness practice
5. Ezekial 45-2, KJV Life in the Spirit Study Bible, copyright 1993,2005 by life publishers International
6. Pierre Teilhard de Chardin,
7. 1 Corinthians 2:12,3:6, KJV Life in the Spirit Study Bible, copyright 1993,2005 by life publishers International
8. John15:11:1-2,1:14,13:2,8:58,7:5,John 15:1,17:5, 15:115:3-11, 15:29
9. Romans 12:13,8:26, KJV Life in the Spirit Study Bible, copyright 1993,2005 by life publishers International
10. Hebrew 1:1, KJV Life in the Spirit Study Bible, copyright 1993,2005 by life publishers International
11. Genesis 1:1,1:3,1:15, 1:1-24, KJV Life in the Spirit Study Bible, copyright 1993,2005 by life publishers International
12. 11Cor.1:4, 2:10-11, KJV Life in the Spirit Study Bible, copyright 1993,2005 by life publishers International

13. 1 John 4:2, 3:8-10,10:23,, KJV Life in the Spirit Study Bible, copyright 1993,2005 by life publishers International
14. Mathew 4:1-3,8:3, 4:1- 11, 13:38-39, KJV Life in the Spirit Study Bible, copyright 1993,2005 by life publishers International
15. Eccesiastic 7:8, KJV Life in the Spirit Study Bible, copyright 1993,2005 by life publishers International
16. Numbers 11:25, KJV Life in the Spirit Study Bible, copyright 1993,2005 by life publishers International
17. Malachi 2:15, KJV Life in the Spirit Study Bible, copyright 1993,2005 by life publishers International
18. www.dictionary.com/browse/residue, KJV Life in the Spirit Study Bible, copyright 1993,2005 by life publishers International
19. Galatians 5:25, KJV Life in the Spirit Study Bible, copyright 1993,2005 by life publishers International
20. Leviticus 11:11, KJV Life in the Spirit Study Bible, copyright 1993,2005 by life publishers International
21. 22.Psalm 139:12,33:6-10, 148:5, KJV Life in the Spirit Study Bible, copyright 1993,2005 by life publishers International
22. 2 Peter 1:21, KJV Life in the Spirit Study Bible, copyright 1993, 2005 by life publishers International
23. Jude 1:20, KJV Life in the Spirit Study Bible, copyright 1993,2005 by life publishers International
24. Exodus 30: 29-32, KJV Life in the Spirit Study Bible, copyright 1993,2005 by life publishers International

25. Luke 8:10-13,22:3-4,21:33, 10:17-20,, KJV Life in the Spirit Study Bible, copyright 1993,2005 by life publishers International
26. Acts 10:38-39, 5:3, 26:16-18, KJV Life in the Spirit Study Bible, copyright 1993,2005 by life publishers International,
27. Eph 4:25-28, 6:11-12, KJV Life in the Spirit Study Bible, copyright 1993,2005 by life publishers International,
28. II Tim 2:25-26, KJV Life in the Spirit Study Bible, copyright 1993,2005 by life publishers International
29. Peter 5:8-9, KJV Life in the Spirit Study Bible, copyright 1993,2005 by life publishers International
30. Rev 12:8-9, 2:8-10 & 2:12-14, KJV Life in the Spirit Study Bible, copyright 1993,2005 by life publishers International
31. I Thes 2:17-19, 2:9-10,KJV Life in the Spirit Study Bible, copyright 1993,2005 by life publishers International,
32. I Tim 5:14-16, KJV Life in the Spirit Study Bible, copyright 1993,2005 by life publishers International
33. Proverbs 18:21, KJV Life in the Spirit Study Bible, copyright 1993,2005 by life publishers International.
34. Ophra.com in her 21 day challenge meditation

CPSIA information can be obtained
at www.ICGtesting.com
Printed in the USA
BVHW07s0057120718
521401BV00001B/46/P